DAY BY DAY WITH JAMES ALLEN

Vic Johnson

Sylvia's Foundation, Inc.
St. Augustine, Florida

Day by Day with James Allen

ISBN: 0-9745717-1-7

Published by
Sylvia's Foundation, Inc.

Distributed by
Executive Books
206 West Allen Street
Mechanicsburg, PA 17055

Printed in the United States of America

Introduction

In 1995 I was attending a business seminar where Charlie "Tremendous" Jones was speaking. He is one of the biggest promoters of the value of reading that I have ever heard. He says, for instance, that you are the same today as you will be in five years except for two things: the books you read and the people you meet. On that day Charlie backed up his belief with the largest "bargain bag" of books I've ever seen. Looking quickly in the bag I could see several books that were of immediate interest, and I easily justified Charlie's "great price."

I pulled out the books of interest and set the rest of the bag aside. When I finally picked *As A Man Thinketh* off my bookshelf several years later, I couldn't put it down. I read it through in one sitting, which isn't too hard to do. The first time through I highlighted the key thoughts. On my second reading I began to underline additional passages that suddenly jumped off the page. By the third reading it was a marked up mess, testifying to the tremendous distillation of wisdom that Allen leaves with us.

There is an oft-used expression "when the student is ready, the teacher will appear." There is no doubt I was ready, and there is no doubt that James Allen was to be my teacher.

In January 2001 I realized a 25-year-old dream to be involved in the personal development industry when I launched www.AsAManThinketh.net with the express purpose of giving away an eBook version of the book that had so influenced me. At this writing we've given away almost 200,000 copies to readers in more than 90 countries.

We also provide our readers a weekly "eMeditation" based on the various writings of Allen. *Day by Day with James Allen* is an edited compendium of some of our most popular "eMeds." Responding to the many requests I've had from subscribers to make these available, we developed the idea of having them published to benefit our favorite charity, Sylvia's Foundation, Inc. 100% of the proceeds of the sale of this book are directed to the Foundation so that it may further its work of "making a difference for young, widowed moms."

I hope its reading will bless your life as much as its writing has blessed mine.

Vic Johnson
Murphy, N.C.
October 28, 2003

First Day of the Month

ACCEPT NO LIMITS

"A person is limited only by the thoughts that he chooses." – *As A Man Thinketh*

You are not limited to the life you now live. It has been accepted by you as the best you can do at this moment. Any time you're ready to go beyond the limitations currently in your life, you're capable of doing that by choosing different thoughts.

We each earn the income we do today because that is the amount we have limited ourselves to earn. We could easily earn 5, 10, 20 times or more if we did not limit ourselves through the thoughts we maintain.

Don't believe that's true? Surely you know people who earn much more than you who don't have your education, your skills, or your intelligence. So why do they earn more than you?

I love the story of George Dantzig that Cynthia Kersey wrote about in *Unstoppable*. As a college student, George studied very hard and always late into the night. So late that he overslept one morning, arriving 20 minutes late for class. He quickly copied the two math problems on the board, assuming they were the homework assignment. It took him several days to work through the two problems, but finally he had a breakthrough and dropped the homework on the professor's desk the next day.

8

Later, on a Sunday morning, George was awakened at 6 a.m. by his excited professor. Since George was late for class, he hadn't heard the professor announce that the two unsolvable equations on the board were mathematical mind teasers that even Einstein hadn't been able to answer. But George Dantzig, working without any thoughts of limitation, had solved not one, but two problems that had stumped mathematicians for thousands of years.

Simply put, George solved the problems because he didn't know he couldn't.

Bob Proctor tells us to "keep reminding yourself that you have tremendous reservoirs of potential within you, and therefore you are quite capable of doing anything you set your mind to. All you must do is figure out how you can do it, not whether or not you can. And once you have made your mind up to do it, it's amazing how your mind begins to figure out how."

And that's worth thinking about.

Second Day of the Month

CONQUER DOUBT

"Thoughts of doubt and fear can never accomplish anything. They always lead to failure."
– *As A Man Thinketh*

There is significant economic evidence that the Great Depression might have been avoided but for the "panic" that swept over the country (and the world) after the 1929 stock market crash. What should have been no more than a deep recession, altered our world forever because of the prevailing "thoughts of doubt and fear."

So great were the thoughts of fear that President Roosevelt felt compelled to deliver a speech about it. By the way, FDR's speech with his now famous, "the only thing we have to fear is fear itself," was suggested to him by Napoleon Hill, author of the classic *Think and Grow Rich*.

If the thoughts of many can bring such great tragedy to our world, is it any wonder that our personal thoughts can do so much damage to our "individual world." When we spend inordinate amounts of time fearing some thing or event in the future, many times that which we fear comes upon us. When it does, we wring our hands in despair and wonder why it had to happen to us, when in reality, we are responsible for our troubles.

Bob Proctor says that the process begins first with a thought of doubt, which causes an emotion of fear, which manifests itself physically as anxiety. Anxiety robs us of our power, our energy and our purpose. Severe anxiety can even undermine our health. And it's all brought on by a thought of doubt.

I have found three things that help me conquer doubt. First, change your mind about the doubt, and keep it changed. If you have a doubt about whether you're going to have enough money to make it to the end of the month, change your mind about it. Whenever the doubt creeps in, affirm to yourself that "I always find a way to have enough of what I need." I love what Emmet Fox says about this, "If you will change your mind concerning anything and absolutely keep it changed, that thing must and will change too. It is the keeping up of the change in thought that is difficult. It calls for vigilance and determination."

The second thing that overcomes fear and doubt is action. "Do the thing you fear and fear will disappear" is more than a nice rhyming aphorism. It's some simple wisdom that always works!

And the third and most important thing to overcoming doubt and fear is Faith. Fear and Faith are directly opposite views of the future and they cannot co-exist. My Faith is in a Creator who has given me dominion over all things. Your Faith may be elsewhere, but know this: Faith and fear cannot be present at the same time.

And that's worth thinking about.

Third Day of the Month

DON'T QUIT

"Your circumstances may be uncongenial, but they shall not remain so if you only perceive an ideal and strive to reach it. You cannot travel within and stand still without."
– *As A Man Thinketh*

For many years I have carried around a poem called *Don't Quit*. One of the lines says, "stick to the fight when you're hardest hit - It's when things seem worst that you mustn't quit." In our darkest hour it's hard to see the end of our circumstance. All we can think of is our conditions worsening. But it's usually at this time that our greatest growth can occur if we'll see the moment as a growth opportunity. If we'll see it as a time to learn how to control our thoughts toward an ideal that we cherish.

One thing I share with people who seek my advice when they think their life has come apart, is to help them understand the power that even the tiniest of actions can have when taken in a negative situation. Remember in Science class when we learned that "a body at rest tends to remain at rest or a body in motion tends to remain in motion." This is especially true when overcoming circumstances because "paralysis" usually keeps us in the condition longer than we'd like.

But even more important, is that once we've started in motion, even though it may not seem like much, know this - it's now only a matter of time before you're out, totally out, of the situation that has got you down today.

My long-time favorite poem by an anonymous author is worth remembering today:

When things go wrong as they sometimes will,
When the road you're trudging seems all uphill.
When the funds are low and the debts are high,
And you want to smile, but you have to sigh.
When care is pressing you down a bit,
Rest if you must, but don't you quit.

Life is queer with its twists and turns,
As everyone of us sometimes learns.
And many a fellow turns about,
When he might have won had he stuck it out.
Don't give up though the pace seems slow,
You may succeed with another blow.

Often the goal is nearer than
It seems to a faint and faltering man.
Often the struggler has given up,
When he might have captured the victor's cup.
And he learned too late when the night came down,
How close he was to the golden crown.

Success is failure turned inside out,
The silver tint of the clouds of doubt.
And you never can tell how close you are,
It may be near when it seems afar.
So stick to the fight when you're hardest hit,
It's when things seem worst that you mustn't quit.

And that's worth thinking about.

Fourth Day of the Month

LIVE IN THE SOLUTION

"A person cannot directly choose his circumstances, but he can choose his thoughts, and so indirectly, yet surely, shape his circumstances." – *As A Man Thinketh*

In her outstanding book, *Choose the Happiness Habit*, Pam Golden writes: "Take the story of two brothers who are twins. One grows up to be an alcoholic bum. The other becomes an extremely successful businessman. When the alcoholic is asked why he became a drunk, he replies, "My father was a drunk." When the successful businessman is asked why he became successful, he says, "My father was a drunk." Same background. Same upbringing. Very different choices."

The brothers chose different thoughts about the identical experience. Those thoughts over the years shaped the circumstances they now find themselves in.

There was a time in my life when I chose to think about challenges and obstacles as just more of the "bad luck" I seemed to attract. Ever hear the expression "when it rains, it pours?" That was my constant mantra when others asked me how things were going. So what do you think I got more of? If you answered "RAIN," you're correct!

Bob Proctor says "you're either living in the problem or you're living in the solution." Now, when

14

I'm confronted with what I used to think was a negative situation, I use a different thought process. I force myself to replace those negative thoughts that creep in with positive thoughts about how I might solve the "problem." Sometimes I'll take a notepad and just start jotting down ideas that might be a solution. At the same time, my thoughts are focused on the possible lessons I might learn from the situation so that I might profit from the experience in the future.

If you've guessed that it doesn't "rain" as much in my life as it used to, you're correct again. In fact, most days it's a beautiful, cloudless and sunny day! Only occasionally now do I get any rain, and it's good rain, the kind that makes living things grow.

And that's worth thinking about.

Fifth Day of the Month

READ THE RIGHT BOOKS

"People are anxious to improve their circumstances, but are unwilling to improve themselves; they therefore remain bound."
– *As A Man Thinketh*

We spend thousands of dollars a year for clothing, cosmetics and other items to change or improve our outward appearance but very little money or time to change our inward condition. Many people easily spend an hour a day brushing, flossing, bathing, and shaving the outside, but find every reason in the world not to spend even a few minutes a day improving the inside.

How do you apply what you learn from *As A Man Thinketh*? Since it is our thoughts that determine the life we will have, you must focus on doing those things that will change your thoughts, and nothing is more effective at changing your thoughts than reading the right books.

I first read *As A Man Thinketh* because of Charlie "Tremendous" Jones. I had attended a seminar where he spoke and he had a table set up at the seminar where, among other things, he offered a huge discount on a big bundle of various personal development and self-help books. I bought the big bundle because I'm a sucker for a "good deal." As it turned out, it was one of the best deals of my life, because several years later, when I finally got around to reading the little book, *As A Man Thinketh* literally changed my life.

Here is what Charlie Jones wrote in the Foreword to the book that I purchased: "You are today the same you'll be in five years from now, except for two things: the people you meet and the books you read. The people you meet can't always be with you, but what you read in books can remain with you a lifetime. How often we hear of individuals who began a new era in their lives from the reading of a single book."

Why not start a new habit today? Spend just fifteen minutes every day before going to bed or upon rising, and read from a personal development book or biography of someone you admire. At the end of a year you will have read about 12 books - at the end of five years about 60 books!! Through your changed thoughts you will have become much more like the "vision you enthrone in your heart."

As English writer Aldous Huxley observed, "Every person who knows how to read has it in his power to magnify himself, to multiply the ways in which he exists, to make his life full, significant, and interesting."

And that's worth thinking about.

Sixth Day of the Month

RELEASE THE PAST

"Do not dwell upon the sins and mistakes of yesterday so exclusively as to have no energy and mind left for living rightly today, and do not think that the sins of yesterday can prevent you from living purely today." - *Byways of Blessedness*

It's been said that the majority of conversations by men over 40 are about the past. Sometimes it's about the "good old days" and sometimes it's about the deals gone bad, the "if I only had" stories, the missed opportunities, etc.

Letting our "sins and mistakes of yesterday" dominate our thinking today robs us of our present joy and our future happiness. It causes us to miss the real opportunity of TODAY!

John Maxwell, in his outstanding best seller, *Failing Forward*, gives some great practical advice: "To move forward today, you must learn to say good-bye to yesterday's hurts, tragedies and baggage. You can't build a monument to past problems and fail forward.

Take time right now to list the negative events from your past that may still be holding you hostage. For each item you list, go through the following exercise:

1. Acknowledge the pain.
2. Grieve the loss.
3. Forgive the person.

18

4. Forgive yourself.
5. Determine to release the event and move on."

Your best days are definitely ahead of you if you treat your "mistakes" as necessary lessons to be learned. If you understand that each lesson brings with it a certain amount of wisdom, you can understand how truly enhanced your life is becoming. Many people can't achieve the success of their dreams because they won't leave their past behind. They won't tear down the monuments they've built to their old hurts and problems.

One of the best teachings I've ever heard on this was from a motivational speaker whose name has escaped me, but whose message didn't: "In life there are no mistakes, only lessons."

And that's worth thinking about.

Seventh Day of the Month

SOWING AND REAPING

"Good thoughts and actions can never produce bad results; bad thoughts and actions can never produce good results. This is but saying that nothing can come from corn but corn, nothing from nettles but nettles."
– *As A Man Thinketh*

Most everyone understands the biblical concept of sowing and reaping because we can grasp the simplicity of the logic. If we were to plant corn in our backyard garden we wouldn't expect spinach to come up. But even though we can grasp the logic, we don't always act as if we understand the power of this principle. And we certainly don't act as if this principle will affect us.

An example: For many years my morning ritual began with a thorough reading of the newspaper, most days spending an hour or more before dashing off to the office. I did not know then that our minds are most impressionable immediately upon rising in the morning and just before sleep in the evening.

Fresh from the reading (and thoughts) of the day's murders, indictments, invasions by foreign dictators, and all other manner of "news", it shouldn't have come as a surprise to me that my sowing of these thoughts would reap an "attitude" toward the rush hour drivers who were "conspiring" to slow down my arrival at work. Thus, by the time I did arrive, I had set the tone for my day, and it was not a positive one.

I gave up my morning ritual ten years ago and replaced it with a ritual of reading and meditating on some works that will sow "good thoughts" and thus reap "good results." I wasn't aware at the time that this was some sound advice offered up by the Apostle Paul, who wrote, "Fix your thoughts on what is true and good and right. Think about things that are pure and lovely, and dwell on the fine, good things in others. Think about all you can praise God for and be glad about."

We always reap what we sow and that is especially true with our thoughts. As Emmet Fox writes, "The secret of life then is to control your mental states, for if you will do this the rest will follow. To accept sickness, trouble, and failure as unavoidable, and perhaps inevitable, is folly, because it is this very acceptance by you that keeps these evils in existence. Man is not limited by his environment. He creates his environments by his beliefs and feelings. To suppose otherwise is like thinking that the tail can wag the dog."

And that's worth thinking about.

Eighth Day of the Month

SEE YOURSELF SUCCEED

"Change of diet will not help a person who will not change his thoughts. When a person makes his thoughts pure, he no longer desires impure food."
– As A Man Thinketh

It's a sad fact that obesity has become a major health threat as it has reached epidemic proportions according to the U.S. Center for Disease Control. Despite the epidemic, the vast majority of those on a weight-loss diet today will fail.

Even sadder is that virtually 100% of the people who fail won't know the REAL reason for their failure. Many will blame the diet they chose, the circumstances in their life, their "lack of willpower," and on and on. But the REAL reason --- the ONLY reason --- they won't succeed is because they didn't change their thoughts. Their thoughts about themselves and the food they eat.

In *Your Winner's Image*, Bob Proctor quotes his mentor Leland Val Vandewall when he writes, "Thinking creates an image. Images control feelings. Feelings cause actions. Actions create results."

I have fought the battle of weight control my entire life. In the last few years I've been mostly winning the battle. During the times when I was losing the battle, it's because of what I thought about myself and what I thought about food. It was easy to fall into the thoughts of the fat, little boy who used to be

22

teased by his playmates. It was even easier to think of food (albeit subconsciously) as an "anesthetic" for the bad feelings created by all my wrong thinking. What a vicious circle.

As each year passes I am even more firmly convinced that you will NEVER achieve sustainable success that exceeds the image you have of yourself. Until you "see" yourself as a healthy, physically-fit person you've got about as much chance of losing weight (and keeping it off!) as you do of making it through this month without receiving any spam.

And this isn't just about weight control. It applies to changing any habit. More than a decade ago I quit a three-pack-a-day cigarette habit. I've never wanted another cigarette – have never even come close to considering it - even though I had tried to quit many times before.

What was the difference? What I thought about myself. Until I quit for good, I always saw myself as a smoker and, of course, I thought like a smoker.

One of Bob's favorite quotes of James Allen says it all:

"Mind is the Master power that moulds and makes,
And Man is Mind, and evermore he takes,
The tool of Thought, and shaping what he wills,
Brings forth a thousand joys, a thousand ills;
He thinks in secret, and it comes to pass;
Environment is but his looking-glass."

And that's worth thinking about.

Ninth Day of the Month

SUFFERING IS A RESPONSE TO PAIN

"Suffering is always the effect of wrong thought in some direction. It is an indication that the individual is out of harmony with himself, with the law of his being." – *As A Man Thinketh*

Most people associate suffering with pain, be it physical, mental or spiritual. They assume suffering to be an automatic result of all pain. However, suffering is not a result of pain, it's a RESPONSE to pain.

Pain is an unpleasant signal that is warning you that something is wrong. Suffering, on the other hand, results from our wrong thinking about the pain. And, in fact, many people experience suffering who have no pain at all (hypochondria is an example of this).

I recently saw Christopher Reeve (he was *Superman* in the movies) being interviewed by Larry King. In May 1995 the one-time "man of steel" was in a riding accident that left him paralyzed from the shoulders down and dependent on a ventilator. It was obvious in watching him, with a drawn face and tense speech, that he has endured and continues to endure an incredible amount of pain. However, his response to this pain has been anything but suffering from it. He has instead devoted his life to helping others, especially those with paralysis. And his accomplishments have been extraordinary.

24

While Christopher has experienced the pain of physical paralysis, many of us have experienced the pain of divorce, layoffs, financial disaster, self-doubt, fear and a host of other ills. But like Reeve, we do not have to "suffer" from our pain --- it's our choice. And we don't have to be Superman or Superwoman to deal with it.

Deepak Chopra defines suffering as "that which threatens to make life meaningless." Life is meaningless when we don't have direction, a goal, or a vision. That's when we are inviting suffering into our life.

Christopher Reeve says, "My feeling is you have to deal with the reality as it is, but not accept it as permanent. I'm sorry, but I just don't believe there is any reason to give up. The goal is a cure. The goal is to get up and out of the wheelchair. And in the meantime, you deal with reality. But if you don't have a vision, nothing happens."

And that's worth thinking about.

Tenth Day of the Month

TAKE THE RESPONSIBILITY

"A Person is buffeted by circumstances so long as he believes himself to be the creature of outside conditions." – *As A Man Thinketh*

One of the great weaknesses of our society today is the growing attitude of victimization. Many people claim themselves to be victims of some outside force. "I had to file bankruptcy because of my ex-wife..", "If my company hadn't laid me off...", "If that driver hadn't pulled out in front of me..."

When we are victims of circumstances, or as James Allen says, a "creature of outside conditions", we have no power. We have given over the power in our life to the circumstances. The longer we give power to our circumstances the worse our circumstances become.

In his book, *Above Life's Turmoil*, Allen writes, "You imagine your circumstances as being separate from yourself, but they are intimately related to your thought world. Nothing appears without an adequate cause."

To get control of our circumstances we must first acknowledge personal responsibility for being where we are. That was the hardest part for me because the "victim" in all of us doesn't want to take that responsibility.

When we take the responsibility we must then take control of our thoughts. And, yes, in the beginning that can be hard. It seems sometimes that it's our nature to first think negatively. But that's just because it's the habit we've developed. And like any habit, it can be changed by replacing it with the habit of thinking the right way.

One of my favorite teachers, Emmet Fox, writes: "You are not happy because you are well. You are well because you are happy. You are not depressed because trouble has come to you, but trouble has come because you are depressed. You can change your thoughts and feelings, and then the outer things will change to correspond, and indeed there is no other way of working."

And that's worth thinking about.

Eleventh Day of the Month

FORMULA FOR SUCCESS

"He conceives of, mentally builds up, an ideal condition of life; the vision of a wider liberty and a larger scope take possession of him; unrest urges him to action, and he utilizes all his spare time and means, small though they are, to the development of his latent powers and resources."
– As A Man Thinketh

Read carefully these 52 words and you will find the keys to success in any endeavor.

Allen is describing a young person who is unschooled, mired in poverty and working in unhealthy conditions. He goes on to write that the young person follows the formula above and becomes a person of "world-wide influence and almost un-equaled power." He finishes the story noting that "He has realized the Vision of his youth. He has become one with his Ideal."

It's a formula for success that's so simple that most people might overlook or discount its effect-iveness. And it's built around one guiding principle - what Napoleon Hill called "a definiteness of purpose." That's what creates the unrest that moves us to action. That's what gives us the energy and drive to spend our spare time and means in developing ourselves to achieve at levels we've never reached before.

One prominent study found that 94% of the 3,000 people interviewed had no definite purpose for their lives. Is it any wonder then that so many people reach their twilight years feeling like life has passed them by.

We have the choice to live our life on purpose or without a purpose. Life doesn't make the distinction, it simply rewards our choice. And the rewards may not always be what we had hoped, as this old poem from *Think and Grow Rich* illustrates:

> "I bargained with Life for a penny,
> And Life would pay no more,
> However I begged at evening
> When I counted my scanty store.
>
> For Life is a just employer,
> He gives you what you ask,
> But once you have set the wages,
> Why, you must bear the task.
>
> I worked for a menial's hire,
> Only to learn, dismayed,
> That any wage I had asked of Life,
> Life would have willingly paid."

And that's worth thinking about.

Twelfth Day of the Month

EVERY CIRCUMSTANCE HAS TWO SIDES

"Your difficulty is not contained, primarily, in the situation which gave rise to it, but in the mental state with which you regard that situation and which you bring to bear upon it."
- Byways of Blessedness

It is one of the most difficult lessons to accept, understand and learn.

Circumstances are not negative or positive, circumstances are neutral. It is our thinking, our mental state, our perspective, that makes a circumstance positive or negative.

Bob Proctor does some of the best teaching on this subject, using a universal law he refers to as the Law of Polarity.

"Everything in the universe has its opposite. There would be no inside to a room without an outside. You have a right and left side to your body, a front and a back. Every up has a down and every down has an up. The Law of Polarity not only states that everything has an opposite -- it is equal and opposite. If it was three feet from the floor up to the table, it would be three feet from the table down to the floor. If it is 150 miles from Manchester to London, by law it must be 150 miles from London to Manchester; it could not be any other way.

"If something you considered bad happens in your life, there has to be something good about it. If it was only a little bad, when you mentally work your way around to the other side, you will find it will only be a little good."

During a recent tele-seminar I conducted with Randy Gage, he used a very good example of this. While the flat tire you have seems to be a negative circumstance to you, it's a very positive circumstance for your local tire dealer. Looking even further it's possible that while changing the tire the dealer discovers a much more serious problem that would have cost you a large sum of money if discovered later.

So it's even more clear from Bob's teaching that every circumstance can be viewed two ways. It's the way we view a circumstance that determines it's impact on our thinking and mental state. And we know from James Allen's teaching that that determines the quality of life that we live.

No matter how bad the circumstance appears to be, taking another look, from another perspective, reveals to us the good. Or, as Napoleon Hill, author of the classic *Think and Grow Rich*, wrote, "Every adversity, every failure and every heartache carries with it the seed of an equivalent or a greater benefit."

And that's worth thinking about.

Thirteenth Day of the Month

FOCUS ON IDEAS

"No person can be confronted with a difficulty which he has not the strength to meet and subdue...Every difficulty can be overcome if rightly dealt with; anxiety is, therefore, unnecessary. The task which cannot be overcome ceases to be a difficulty and becomes an impossibility...and there is only one way of dealing with an impossibility - namely to submit to it." - *Byways of Blessedness*

Most people who read these eMeditations probably think that I write them for others. The truth is, I write them for me. I need them as much or more than the folks I write for.

Several days ago when I started this I was confronted with a difficulty that I allowed to fill me with a great deal of anxiety. It's not a new difficulty or even a totally unexpected one. But I was faced with a decision that will have long-term ramifications. One of those kind of decisions that we'd rather not make - one of those decisions that makes you want to pull the covers up over your head in the morning.

James Allen's words are so incredibly penetrating on this subject because he's basically saying that there's no problem that we should be anxious about. We can either solve it or it's impossible to solve. Kind of reminds you of the Serenity Prayer doesn't it? "God grant me the serenity to accept the things I cannot change; courage to change the things I can; and the Wisdom to know the difference."

I once heard Rita Davenport give some great advice on handling most of the problems in our life: "If money can fix it, it's not a problem." Well that's great, you say, but I don't have the money to fix it, so I've got a problem. Wrong thinking. Because the truth is you're only one idea away from obtaining whatever amount of money you might need. So instead of focusing on the money you don't have (which will almost surely result in you attracting more lack into your life), focus on ideas, ideas, ideas.

There's also another great reason not to be anxious about the difficulty you're facing today - it contains a lesson. And once you master it, you will be much stronger and wiser. My long-time hero, Emmet Fox, wrote, "It is the Law that any difficulties that can come to you at any time, no matter what they are, must be exactly what you need most at the moment, to enable you to take the next step forward by overcoming them. The only real misfortune, the only real tragedy, comes when we suffer without learning the lesson."

And that's worth thinking about.

Fourteenth Day of the Month

HARMONIZING THOUGHTS

"A person is the causer (though nearly always unconsciously) of his circumstances, and that, whilst aiming at the good end, he is continually frustrating its accomplishment by encouraging thoughts and desires which cannot possibly harmonize with that end." – *As A Man Thinketh*

One of the examples James Allen uses to support this philosophy is a rich man who is the victim of a painful and persistent disease as the result of gluttony. He's willing to give large sums of money to get rid of the disease and he fully expects that will be the cure. Unfortunately, he never addresses the gluttonous desire that is the cause of his condition. He can never achieve good health because his desires are not in harmony with the good health he seeks, regardless of the money he spends.

Wow, did I relate to the rich man. Not because of his money, but because of his attitude. There's been so many times in my life that I said I wanted to get rid of negative circumstances, all the while I'm engaging in the actions (brought on by my thoughts) that could never possibly harmonize with the result I said I wanted.

Once I remember a big commitment and resolution on my part to spend more time with my family. I optimistically laid out a calendar of activities we would do together and got very excited about the "new me." The way I had it figured, I'd probably be "father of the year."

Well, I'm glad they didn't publish the results of the "competition" that year, I'm sure I would have finished dead last. You see, despite my "aiming at the good end," I hadn't changed the thought patterns that had plagued me for years. Any type of crisis in my business was a justifiable reason for me to work late or to go in on the weekends. While my mouth said that my family was more important, my actions (and thoughts) said otherwise.

James Allen wants us to understand that we cannot change our circumstances without first changing our thoughts to harmonize with the circumstances we want. To think otherwise is just as foolish as the gluttonous rich man.

One of my great enlightenments came from Wayne Dyer's *You'll See It When You Believe It*. He wrote, "Work each day on your thoughts rather than concentrating on your behavior. It is your thinking that creates the feelings you have and ultimately your actions as well."

And that's worth thinking about.

Fifteenth Day of the Month

DREAMS ARE MAGIC SPARKS

"Dreams are the seedlings of realities."
– As A Man Thnketh

Look slowly around you. All that you see at this moment was one day but someone's dream - a "seedling of the reality" it was to become. In our lifetime we have benefited greatly from the dreams of so many.

Mandela, Mother Teresa, Einstein, Gandhi, Spielberg, Disney, Gates, and the list could go on and on and on --- all began with a dream. Who could forget one of the most powerful speeches of all time by Dr. Martin Luther King, *I Have A Dream*. While we haven't become the color-blind society we should be, go back and read the speech and see how far we've come since Dr. King first spoke those "seedlings" into reality.

At the 1996 Atlanta Olympics, Celine Dion performed a song called *The Power Of The Dream*. Some of the lyrics read:

"Deep within each heart,
There lies a magic spark,
That lights the fire of our imagination...

Your mind will take you far,
The rest is just pure heart,
You'll find your fate is all your own creation."

36

Sounds a lot like James Allen, doesn't it?

So maybe you don't see yourself as a Mandela or Mother Teresa. But if you haven't already discovered it, deep inside you there is a dream. It was put there by the one who created you, as we are told in Jeremiah 29:11, "For I know the plans I have for you, plans to give you hope and a future."

Ralph Marston, whose *Daily Motivator* has brightened my day for some time now, writes, "On a regular basis, take time to imagine the very best that life can be. Step aside for a moment from the day-to-day concerns of life. Re-establish contact with your highest goals and most treasured dreams. Remind yourself of the beautiful possibilities that life holds for you. Renew your determination to bring them to fruition.

"Spend some quality time with your dreams. They are real to the extent that you value them. To the extent that you commit to them and work for them, they will come true."

The final verse of Celine's song ends with:

"There's so much strength in all of us,
Every woman, child and man,
It's the moment that you think you can't,
You'll discover that you can."

And that's worth thinking about.

The Power Of The Dream copyright 1996 Celine Dion

Sixteenth Day of the Month

MASTER YOUR FEARS

"Doubt and fear are the great enemies of knowledge, and he who encourages them, who does not slay them, thwarts himself at every step." – *As A Man Thinketh*

I've heard it said that we're born with only a few fears – like the fear of falling and the fear of loud noises. All other fears we learn along the way. Like the fear of failure, the fear of rejection - even a fear of success. I believe our greatest enemy in life is fear, because fear keeps us from doing many of those things we would like to do that would make our life more complete and more enjoyable.

Doubt is the first cousin of fear and precedes it. We weren't born with doubt. Our habit of doubt has grown throughout our life. If we dwell on a doubt and give in to it, it then grows into fear. The Apostle James reminds us that doubt makes us ineffective, "a doubtful mind will be as unsettled as the wave of the sea that is tossed and driven by the wind; and every decision you then make will be uncertain, as you turn first this way, and then that."

If most of our fears and all of our doubts are learned along the way, then we can "unlearn" them by becoming masters of our thoughts. I've heard Zig Ziglar quote Mark Twain when he said, "True courage is not the absence of fear, it's the mastery of fear." The people who live the life of their dreams have just as many fears as those who live miserable, unfulfilled lives - they have just learned to master their fears instead of allowing their fears to master them.

Norman Vincent Peale, writing in *You Can If You Think You Can*, provides us with a prescription for mastering fear and doubt. "You can cancel out fear with faith. For there is no force in this world more powerful than faith. The most amazing things can happen as a result of it...There are two massive thought forces competing for control of the mind: fear and faith, and faith is stronger, much stronger. Hold that thought of faith's greater power until you believe it, for it can be the difference between success and failure."

Ambrose Redmoon said that, "Courage is not the absence of fear, but rather the judgment that something else is more important than fear." Everyone is afraid at some time or another. Those who succeed in conquering fear have put their focus on what's more important to them rather than on the fear. If your young child darted into the street in front of traffic, you'd easily overcome the fear of any physical danger that retrieving the child would pose. The child's life is more important to you than the fear. So focus on what's beyond the fear - what's on the other side - when you overcome the fear.

Brian Tracy has a great way to fight doubt. He says, "Don't wonder whether something is possible - don't get bogged down in WHETHER. Ask HOW. Over and over if you have to, but ask how can you do it, not whether you can."

And that's worth thinking about.

Seventeenth Day of the Month

PERSIST UNTIL

"Great is the heartfelt joy when, after innumerable and apparently unsuccessful attempts, some ingrained fault of character is at last cast out to trouble its erstwhile victim and the world no more."
- The Mastery of Destiny

James Allen is sharing with us the reward (heartfelt joy) for finally overcoming a personal character deficit. However, what he's really sharing with us is the value of persistence.

If I had to pick one character trait that I think is a "must have" in order to be successful in any endeavor, it would be persistence. In fact, it seems to be the one trait that is the dominant trait in every single, super-successful individual I know. I believe it to be the one trait that any ordinary person can use to become extraordinary ("extra-ordinary").

Napoleon Hill, who wrote *Think and Grow Rich*, devoted an entire chapter to Persistence and said that the only thing that was different about Henry Ford and Thomas Edison was their persistence.

I've long since forgotten where I read it, but I've never forgotten the story of the tribe in Africa that confounded all of the anthropologists. It seems that this tribe had for centuries enjoyed a 100% success rate with its rain dance. In comparing this tribe to other tribes who did rain dances but who didn't always experience success, the experts couldn't find anything that differentiated the one tribe. They performed the same rituals, praying the same incantations to the same gods, in the same costumes. Like all the tribes, they sometimes danced for days, even weeks on end. Finally an astute observer noticed something very telling. The successful tribe did one thing - and only one thing - different than the other tribes. It ALWAYS danced UNTIL it rained!

If your head is hanging low today as mine has done on many a day, I hope you'll find the encouragement to know that you really only need to do one thing at this point --- PERSIST. And that means taking just one step in the right direction --- even a half step in the right direction.

Yes, maybe you need to review your plan or change your plan or maybe you even need to create a plan in the first place :-) But the one way you can ensure that you will meet with success (it's absolutely guaranteed) -- is to "dance until it rains!"

And that's worth thinking about.

Eighteenth Day of the Month

DEFINITELY DIRECTED THOUGHT

"All achievements, whether in the business, intellectual, or spiritual world, are the result of definitely directed thought."
- As A Man Thinketh

How many times have you heard the expression that most people spend more time planning their vacation than they do planning their life. I would expand that expression by adding that most people spend more time "thinking" about their vacation than they do thinking about what's important in their life.

The power of "definitely directed thought" (the power of purpose) is why I love the story of John Goddard so much.

When he was fifteen-years-old, Goddard was inspired to create a list of 127 "life goals." By one count, the "young seventy-something" has accomplished 109 of these PLUS 300 others he set along the way!!

Here's just a few of the ones he's reached:

He climbed the Matterhorn, Ararat, Kilimanjaro, Fiji, Rainier and the Grand Tetons.

He retraced the route of Marco Polo through all of the Middle East, Asia and China and was the first man to explore the whole length of the world's longest river, the Nile. He also boated down the Amazon, Congo and others.

He has been to 120 countries, explored the underwater reefs of Florida, the Great Barrier Reef in Australia, the Red Sea, visited the Great Wall of China, the Okefenokee Swamp in Georgia, and the Everglades of Florida.

He has flown 47 different types of aircraft, and set several civilian air-speed records including one at 1,500 miles an hour. He flew an F-106 to an altitude of 63,000 feet, making him the only civilian to pilot an aircraft that high, a record which he still holds.

And I'm just getting started. But I think you get the point.

Okay, maybe it's been awhile since you were fifteen, and maybe coming up with 127 life goals is a bit intimidating at this point. But how about 10? How much would the quality of your life improve if you accomplished just one life goal in each of the next ten years?

You won't ever know if you don't start now --- and you don't WRITE them down.

More than just one of the greatest adventurers the world has ever known, Goddard is an incredibly wise person, as this quote of his demonstrates: "If you really know what you want out of life, it's amazing how opportunities will come to enable you to carry them out."

And that's worth thinking about.

Nineteenth Day of the Month

GOOD THOUGHTS BEAR GOOD FRUIT

"Every thought-seed sown or allowed to fall into the mind, and to take root there, produces its own, blossoming sooner or later into act, and bearing its own fruitage of opportunity and circumstance. Good thoughts bear good fruit, bad thoughts bad fruit." - *As A Man Thinketh*

My friend, Mark Shearon, once posed a very enlightening question to a telephone audience, "Are you thinking about what you're thinking about?" Read that sentence again and read it carefully. It's not a play on words.

Most people give very little thought to what occupies their thinking and even fewer people understand that "good thoughts bear good fruit, bad thoughts, bad fruit." Most of us understand the law of sowing and reaping in other aspects of life, but we fail to understand that this same law is just as potent when our thoughts are involved.

A June 1997 story in the *Wall Street Journal* said that HMOs reported that as much as 70 percent of all visits to a primary care physician are for a psycho-somatic illness -- a disorder that involves both mind and body. According to Dr. David Sobel, a primary care physician and author of the highly respected *Mind-Body Health Newsletter*, only 16 percent of people who visit their physician for common maladies like nausea, headache and stomach upset are diagnosed with a physical, organic cause. That means that a whopping 84% are suffering from an illness that originated in THOUGHT!

These statistics tell us that the majority of people literally think their way to sickness.

If you've never trained yourself in "right thinking," I challenge you to spend today monitoring and recording your thoughts. If you understand the power of thought in your life, at the end of the day you won't be surprised at why your life is where it's at today, be it good or bad.

In *Make Your Life Worthwhile*, Emmet Fox wrote, "The more you think about lack, bad times, etc., the worse will your business be; and the more you think of prosperity, abundance, and success, the more of these things will you bring into your life.

The more you think about your grievances or the injustices that you have suffered, the more such trials will you continue to receive; and the more you think of the good fortune you have had, the more good fortune will come to you."

And that's worth thinking about.

Twentieth Day of the Month

BE BLIND TO FAILURE

"He who cherishes a beautiful vision, a lofty ideal in his heart, will one day realize it."
- As A Man Thinketh

There was an incredible story in the June 18, 2001 issue of *Time* magazine about Erik Weihenmayer who had recently climbed Mt. Everest.

Now there's been quite a few people that have climbed the world's highest summit since Sir Edmund Hillary first did it in 1953. But no one had ever climbed Mt. Everest that was blind, until Erik Weihenmayer did.

What's even more amazing is that on September 5, 2002 he reached the top of Mt. Kosciusko, the highest peak in Australia. That made Erik the first blind climber to reach the top of the traditional Seven Summits, the most challenging peaks in the world.

Erik can't see like most of us can, but he knows, like James Allen knew, that if we settle for what we can see today, we'll never live the life of our dreams. We have to have a vision for our life, for what we want to become. Most importantly, we have to cherish it and hold on tightly to it when circumstances are telling us that we'll never see our vision.

If you read Erik's story you'll discover that Erik stumbled into the Camp on the first floor of Mt. Everest bloodied, sick and dehydrated. And he was still 9,000 feet (almost two miles) from the summit. But Erik had cherished and lived with his vision for years and would not be denied. Like the title of the story says, Erik was "blind to failure."

The ancient writer tells us in Proverbs that "Without a vision, the people perish." So we must take the time to determine the vision for our life. But once we've settled on our vision, then it's important that we take James Allen's advice to cherish it in our heart.

And, as Erik says, "Success is not just the crowning moment, the spiking of the ball in the end zone or the raising of the flag on the summit. It is the whole process of reaching for a goal and, sometimes, it begins with failure."

And that's worth thinking about.

Twenty-first Day of the Month

DECIDE TO GROW

"Only by much searching and mining are gold and diamonds obtained, and a person can find every truth connected with his being, if he will dig deep into the mine of his soul." - *As A Man Thinketh*

The classic book *Acres of Diamonds* is the story of a person who sold his home and land to travel far and wide in search of diamonds, only to die penniless. As the story goes, the new owner discovered diamonds on the very property that the old owner had ignored.

A lot of times I think we act the same way when we're trying to "fix" something in our life. Whether it's happiness or self-esteem or love that we seek, many times we look outside of ourselves to find the answer. We look to a spouse, a friend, a child or a parent to fill the void. Perhaps we expect the answer to come from our pursuit of our occupation or other interests. Or we expect a new home, a new car or a new boat to satisfy our "hunger."

But, alas, like the poor farmer in *Acres of Diamonds*, our search comes up empty handed. And just like the story, diamonds are waiting to be discovered in our own back yard. As James Allen points out, the only way to find the gold and diamonds is to "dig deep into the mine of the soul." It is here, he says, that we will find EVERY TRUTH connected to our being.

48

One of my most favorite authors, Jim Rohn, says, "The greatest source of unhappiness comes from inside." Conversely, that's also where the greatest (and only) source of true happiness comes from.

Instead of searching far and wide, spend some time every day searching inside. Instead of expecting something outside to fill you up, learn to fill yourself from within. Make a commitment to read more of the material that will help you discover who you are. Make a decision to grow. As Jim Rohn also says, "What you become directly influences what you get."

And that's worth thinking about.

Twenty-second Day of the Month

CREATE YOUR OWN CIRCUMSTANCES

"A person only begins to become the person he wants to be when he ceases to whine and revile, and commences to search for the hidden justice which regulates his life." - *As A Man Thinketh*

I had to look up the meaning of the word revile because I've never seen it used. It means to condemn, despise, berate. I didn't have to look up the meaning of the word whine. In fact I'm sure some of my friends have sometimes wanted to ask me if I "wanted some cheese with that whine?"

When we whine and revile we give power to that which we revile and whine about. We cease to be in charge of our life. I love the way that Wayne Dyer describes it in *You'll See It When You Believe It*. He says, "I no longer view the world in terms of unfortunate accidents or misfortunes. I know in my being that I influence it all, and now find myself considering why I created a situation, rather than saying, "why me?" This heightened awareness directs me to look inside of myself for answers. I take responsibility for all of it, and the interesting puzzle becomes a fascinating challenge when I decide to influence areas of my life in which I previously believed I was not in control. I now feel that I control it all."

One of my favorite quotes on this subject is from George Bernard Shaw. "People are always blaming their circumstances for what they are. I don't believe in circumstances. The people who get on in the world are the people who get up and look for the circumstances they want, and if they can't find them, make them."

So how do we develop the necessary character to make our circumstances instead of allowing our circumstances to make us. Emmet Fox tells us that "you can build any quality into your mentality by meditating upon that quality every day. If you seem to yourself to be lacking in certain necessary qualities, if your character seems to lack strength, ask God to give you what you need - and He will."

And that's worth thinking about.

Twenty-third Day of the Month

YOUR THOUGHTS BROUGHT YOU HERE

"You are today where your thoughts have brought you; you will be tomorrow where your thoughts take you." - *Above Life's Turmoil*

This principle was not easy for me to accept and I fought it for a long time. As miserable as my life was at the time I learned this concept, I was certain that there was no way that it was due to the thoughts that I had held. There were too many other reasons why things had gone bad: my ex-spouse, the economy, a client who had wronged me, and on and on and on. Since I wasn't responsible for my "bad luck," then certainly my thoughts had nothing to do with it.

But I was wrong. Like the biblical Job who said, "the thing I feared most has come upon me," I, too, had thought myself to the situation I was in.

Dr. Walter Doyle Staples, writing in *Think Like a Winner!* says, "I credit one simple concept with getting me started on my journey into self-discovery. After a great deal of study and contemplation, I came to the conclusion that people have in their lives today exactly what they keep telling their mind they want."

Like Dr. Staples, it was a moment of great illumination for me! The logical side of me said, "if you and you alone can think yourself into such a mess, then surely you and you alone can think yourself out of it."

And that I did. It wasn't overnight and it wasn't easy, but it was a sure thing! And by accepting all of the responsibility for where I was, and all of the responsibility for where I was going, I experienced a tremendous joy and freedom. I knew in my knower that if I got myself into the predicament, I could get myself out.

Of course, I had some great inspiration along the way. And I will always remember Les Brown's three steps to take during "hard times:"

1. Have Faith (didn't Paul say, "Faith is the substance of things hoped for...")
2. Remind yourself: "No matter how hard it is or how hard it gets, I'm going to make it!"
3. Have patience and engage in consistent action.

And that's worth thinking about.

Twenty-fourth Day of the Month

PROBLEMS BRING LESSONS

"As a progressive and evolving being, man is where he is that he may learn that he may grow; and as he learns the spiritual lesson which any circumstance contains for him, it passes away and gives place to other circumstances."
- As A Man Thinketh

It has taken me a long time to be able to look at a problem I'm having as a necessary spiritual lesson. To be frank, I'm still not always really excited to be enduring the pain and frustration that negative circumstances usually cause. Some days I'd like to "play hookey" and skip the lesson :-)

But as I look back at my life, it is easy to see that the times when my wisdom and understanding grew to new levels; those times when I approached becoming the person I long to be; it was always the times that followed negative circumstances. The greatest growth you're going to have is going to come from the negative circumstance you have today that sometimes seems too overwhelming, too big to scale.

Writing in *Byways of Blessedness*, James Allen is strong in his call for us to embrace our circumstances. "Let a person rejoice when he is confronted with obstacles, for it means that he has reached the end of some particular line of indifference or folly, and is now called upon to summon up all his energy and intelligence in order to extricate himself, and to find a better way; that the powers within him are crying out for greater freedom, for enlarged exercise and scope.

"No situation can be difficult of itself; it is the lack of insight into its intricacies, and the want of wisdom in dealing with it, which give rise to the difficulty. Immeasurable, therefore, is the gain of a difficulty transcended."

Maybe that explains why it sometimes seems that I can't shake a particular problem, or I have one that keeps rearing its ugly head. Instead of fighting it, I need to jump in and gain the insight and wisdom to handle it. Then it would be gone, and I would be ready for the next lesson -- only stronger, both in spirit and in wisdom!

And that's worth thinking about.

Twenty-fifth Day of the Month

BELIEVE IT'S POSSIBLE

"Belief is the basis of all action, and, this being so, the belief that dominates the hearts or mind is shown in the life." - *Above Life's Turmoil*

You will rarely attempt something you don't believe possible and you will NEVER give 100% of your ability to something you don't believe in.

Some years ago I was listening to a friend speaking to a business audience. She quoted a teaching by David Schwartz from *The Magic of Thinking Big* that rocked my life. She said, "The size of your success is determined by the size of your belief." Now that was the first personal development book I ever read and I've read it at least 20 times since. I'm sure that I had heard that concept many times before that night. But it impacted me so much that I wrote it down and must have looked at it a hundred times or more in the thirty days after that.

I spent the next few months focused on strengthening my belief in myself and in what I wanted to do. I took to heart what Wayne Dyer wrote in *You'll See It When You Believe It*: "Work each day on your thoughts rather than concentrating on your behavior. It is your thinking that creates the feelings that you have and ultimately your actions as well." So I worked each day on my beliefs by constantly affirming myself using written and verbal affirmations. The years since have been an incredible rocket ride.

One of the best known stories about the power of belief is about Roger Bannister, the first person to run a mile in under four minutes. Before his accomplishment it was generally believed that the human body was incapable of such a feat. But as soon as he had done it, scores of others accomplished the same thing. Thousands have done so since and today it's not uncommon for it to be done by a talented high-schooler. Did the human body change so that this could be done? No. But the human belief system did!

Nightingale-Conant says Napoleon Hill is considered to have influenced more people into success than any other person in history. And his most quoted line from *Think and Grow Rich* describes the power of belief: "Whatever your mind can conceive and believe, it can achieve." Just believing that statement, truly believing it deep down inside, is a bold step toward living your dreams.

Lisa Jimenez, in her great book *Conquer Fear!* writes, "Change your beliefs and you change your behaviors. Change your behaviors and you change your results. Change your results and you change your life."

And that's worth thinking about.

Twenty-sixth Day of the Month

PERSISTENCE GROWS YOUR ROOT SYSTEM

"The person of good and lawful purpose cannot fail. It only needs that he daily renew the fire and energy of his fixed resolve, to consummate his object." - *The Mastery of Destiny*

It is the great equalizer for all of those reaching for success. It overcomes lack of education, money, talent, intelligence, looks and all other seeming advantages. President Calvin Coolidge said nothing could take its place: "Persistence and determination alone are omnipotent."

I cannot think of one victory I've ever had that I won without persistence. For a while I just thought that I had to work harder and longer than anyone else in order to achieve because nothing has ever come easy for me. Then I really looked around and noticed that everyone else was just like me. Every mentor I've ever had and every successful person I've ever known has their own story of how persistence was the key to their success.

Here's what Bob Proctor teaches on one of the Universal Laws called the Law of Gender: "This law decrees that all seeds (ideas are spiritual seeds) have a gestation or incubation period before they manifest. In other words, when you choose a goal or build the image in your mind, a definite period of time must elapse before that image manifests in physical results."

One of my most favorite inspirational examples about persistence is the story of an Asian Bamboo species that even after five years of watering, weeding and fertilizing is barely visible. Then, in a span of about six weeks, it grows two and a half feet a day to 90 feet and higher. It grows so fast that you can literally "hear" it growing. The question to ask is did the bamboo grow 90 feet in six weeks or did it grow 90 feet in five years?

Obviously it grew 90 feet in five years, for all the time when growth wasn't visible it was developing a massive root system that would later support its magnificent growth.

Can you see where the current circumstances in your life are developing your massive root system? Can you see where you must continue to "fertilize" and "water" yourself even though maybe you can't see any visible changes today?

Napoleon Hill thought that persistence was such a key to success that he devoted an entire chapter to it in the classic *Think and Grow Rich.* He writes, "Persistence is a state of mind, therefore it can be cultivated....Before success comes in any person's life, he is sure to meet with much temporary defeat, and, perhaps, some failure. When defeat overtakes a person, the easiest and most logical thing to do is to QUIT. That is exactly what the majority of people do. More than five hundred of the most successful people this country has ever known told the author their greatest success came just one step beyond the point at which defeat had overtaken them."

And that's worth thinking about.

Twenty-seventh Day of the Month

IDENTIFY YOUR VISION

"The vision that you glorify in your mind, the ideal that you enthrone in your heart - this you will build your life by; this you will become."
- As A Man Thinketh

Whether you liked his politics or not, much can be learned from the life of former President Clinton. Grolier's *New Book of Knowledge* reports that as a teenager "Clinton thought of becoming a doctor or a reporter or even a musician. But after a fateful meeting with President John F. Kennedy, while still in high school, he made up his mind to enter politics." At that moment a vision was born that he would hold onto - that he would glorify in his mind over and over - for the next 30 years, until he himself was elected President at the age of 46.

Jay Leno, who succeeded the venerable Johnny Carson as host of *The Tonight Show*, first envisioned that he would be the host when he was just 22-years-old and unknown and unproven as a comedian, much less as host of a show of such regard. For twenty years he enthroned in his heart an ideal that most people would have thought was "foolish", "outlandish" and "impossible."

Thoreau told us that "The mass of men lead lives of quiet desperation." No doubt it's because the masses are without a vision for their lives.

60

What is your vision for your future, your ideal life? Is it written down? Do you review it and think about it often? Have you "enthroned" it in your heart? Is your life organized around goals and objectives that will ensure your vision is reached?

Wallace D. Wattles wrote, "There is no labor from which most people shrink as they do from that of sustained and consecutive thought; it is the hardest work in the world." And yet it is the "sustained and consecutive thought" about our vision that is the first and primary labor of achievement.

Thoreau also wrote one of my most favorite passages of all time. And it gives you the best reason there is to stop what you're doing today and identify the vision for your life. "If one advances confidently in the direction of his dreams, and endeavors to live the life which he has imagined, he will meet with a success unexpected in common hours."

And that's worth thinking about.

Twenty-eighth Day of the Month

THOUGHTS CREATE BEHAVIOR

"Cause and effect are as absolute and undeviating in the hidden realm of thought as in the world of visible and material things." – *As A Man Thinketh*

We remember from science class Newton's physical law that "every action creates an equal and opposite reaction." Or, every cause has an effect. And because it is a law, it is absolute and undeviating. It always happens - in every circumstance, under every condition.

James Allen says the same law that applies in the physical also applies in the world of thought. Every effect must have an originating cause. Our life does not develop as a result of chance but as a result of causes.

In the thought world, a thought (the cause) creates a feeling (the effect). Feelings can eventually materialize in the physical world because they create actions or behavior. These actions cause results or outcomes, and thus our life goes.

When we say a person "looks worried" what has taken place? A negative thought of some kind (the cause) triggered a feeling of worry (the effect) that materialized in the physical world through the person's facial actions. Those feelings may also materialize in other ways. For instance, by increased blood pressure or nausea. All of these "effects" originated from the original cause which was a thought.

62

Dr. Wayne Dyer writes that "all of our behavior results from the thoughts that preceded it...so the thing to work on is not your behavior but the thing that caused your behavior, your thoughts."

That was so liberating to me because I was so frustrated in trying to change the behaviors that I knew were causing the pain in my life. But I had been working on the wrong thing.

We cannot change anything in our life without first changing the originating cause. And everything in our life originates in our thoughts.

As Jim Rohn says: "if the idea of having to change ourselves makes us uncomfortable, we can remain as we are. We can choose rest over labor, entertainment over education, delusion over truth, and doubt over confidence. The choices are ours to make. But while we curse the effect, we continue to nourish the cause."

And that's worth thinking about.

Twenty-ninth Day of the Month

CONTROL YOUR DESTINY

"A person is literally what he thinks, his character being the complete sum of all his thoughts."
- As A Man Thinketh

James Allen means character in both the broad and narrow sense; our total being in the broad sense and our moral fiber in the narrow sense.

We are where we are today because of all the thoughts we have had up until today. Where we are in the future will be based on the thoughts we accumulate until that day. Through our thoughts we have created the life we live. And that was probably as hard for me to accept as any thing I've encountered because I didn't want to admit that the garbage in my life had been my own creation.

But I learned something very valuable when I really analyzed this concept. If it was my thinking, and my thinking alone, that had brought me such a miserable condition, then Hallelujah! I could change my thinking and change my condition.

And it was true --- and it worked. And it continues to work!

He's not talking about the fleeting thoughts that come into our mind and disappear quickly. He's talking about the thoughts we dwell on, the ones we return to over and over.

64

Maybe it's the past negative circumstances that we've built personal monuments to. Maybe it's a negative thought about some aspect of our health or finances, and we keep returning to this thought again and again. Or perhaps it's some wrong we've suffered at the hands of someone who used to be close to us. It's these thoughts that shape our lives in ways that bring us misery and unhappiness.

How devastating if we look back at our life with regret. Doesn't that act of looking back create another thought (or thoughts)? Doesn't that affect our life today and tomorrow?

On the other hand, how exhilarating it is if we look forward with confidence. If we accept James Allen's philosophy it means that we each alone control our destiny. William James, the great psychologist of the early Twentieth Century, said the greatest discovery of his generation was that people could choose their destiny.

It's not our circumstances, not our spouse, not our boss. It's our thoughts that are in control! So we can be in control...because we can control our thoughts.

And that's worth thinking about.

Thirtieth Day of the Month

THE POWER OF FAITH

"By the power of faith every enduring work is accomplished. Faith in the Supreme, faith in the overruling Law; faith in your work, and in your power to accomplish that work - here is the rock upon which you must build if you would achieve, if you would stand and not fall."
– Path to Prosperity

James Allen makes a pretty bold claim: "By the power of faith every enduring work is accomplished." He doesn't say some enduring works or many enduring works, but EVERY enduring work.

A Duke University research study, among many others, found a link between religious faith and illness prevention, coping and recovery. Those with a strong faith tended to be ill less often and when they were ill tended to recover more quickly. We all know stories of people who experienced some type of miracle in their life because they had the faith all along that they would.

In *Think and Grow Rich*, the number one success classic of all time, Napoleon Hill wrote the following about the power of faith: "Faith is the "eternal elixir" which gives life, power and action to the impulse of thought! Faith is the starting point of all accumulation of riches! Faith is the basis of all "miracles" and all mysteries which cannot be analyzed by the rules of science! Faith is the only known antidote for failure!"

Realize that the only things that can keep us from having the kind of faith that Allen and Hill describe are fear, doubt and worry. These are the opposite of faith.

Fear that your car won't start this morning, that you're going to be in the next group of layoffs, that you can't possibly save enough now to ever retire. Doubts that you'll ever own that business you've always wanted, that your children will grow into happy, well adjusted adults. Worry that you won't have enough money to make it until the end of the month, that the medical test is going to come back with bad news. The list goes on and on.

Fear, doubt and worry rob us of a real life and keep us from moving forward. But more than anything, they rob us of faith - and without faith we are powerless.

How do we overcome fear, doubt and worry in order to maintain faith? Hill says that "Repetition of affirmation of orders to your subconscious mind is the only known method of voluntary development of the emotion of faith." In other words, we can literally think and talk ourselves into faith just as easily as we think and talk ourselves into fear, doubt and worry.

And that's worth thinking about.

Thirty-first Day of the Month

THE MAGIC IS IN YOU

"When he realizes that he is a creative power, and that he may command the hidden soil and seeds of his being out of which circumstances grow; he then becomes the rightful master of himself."
– As A Man Thinketh

I was reading an old classic the other day, *The Message of a Master* by John McDonald, and I was rocked by an incredibly insightful passage: "The cause of the confusion prevailing in your mind that weakens your thoughts is the false belief that there is a power or powers outside you greater than the power within you."

Stop and think about that. What keeps us from attempting greater things -- from reaching for the brass ring in our life? What makes us take that great idea that could make our family financially free and bury it underneath a lot of reasons why it'd never work? What stops us from that career change that would result in working in a profession we could really enjoy, could get passionate about?

There's only one thing that EVER stops us from forward momentum and McDonald nailed it: "the false belief that there is a power or powers outside you greater than the power within you."

As I once heard a speaker say, "The magic is in YOU!" As James Allen tells us, once we realize that we can create our circumstances, then, and only then, are we truly the master of our life and our destiny.

Regardless of your particular spiritual beliefs, you may find these words from the Gospel of John very enlightening, "He that believeth on me, the works that I do, shall he do also; and greater works than these shall he do." That would indicate to me that we are already "endowed" with the power to do amazing things -- far more amazing than most of us will ever attempt -- if we'd only understand and BELIEVE that the power is within, not without.

And that's worth thinking about.

As A Man Thinketh

James Allen

Foreword

This little volume (the result of meditation and experience) is not intended as an exhaustive treatise on the much-written-upon subject of the power of thought. It is suggestive rather than explanatory, its object being to stimulate men and women to the discovery and perception of the truth that "They themselves are makers of themselves" by virtue of the thoughts which they choose and encourage; that mind is the master weaver, both of the inner garment of character and the outer garment of circumstance, and that, as they may have hitherto woven in ignorance and pain they may now weave in enlightenment and happiness.

James Allen
Ilfracombe, England

Editor's Note: James Allen wrote As A Man Thinketh over 100 years ago. We know that were he to write it today that it would be gender-neutral. To respect the integrity of the author's work we have maintained the gender references that appear in his original manuscript.

Thought And Character

The aphorism, "As a man thinketh in his heart, so is he," not only embraces the whole of a man's being, but is so comprehensive as to reach out to every condition and circumstance of his life. A man is literally what he thinks, his character being the complete sum of all his thoughts.

As the plant springs from, and could not be without, the seed, so every act of man springs from the hidden seeds of thought, and could not have appeared without them. This applies equally to those acts called "spontaneous" and "unpremeditated" as to those which are deliberately executed.

Act is the blossom of thought, and joy and suffering are its fruit; thus does a man garner in the sweet and bitter fruitage of his own husbandry.

Thought in the mind hath made us.
What we are by thought was wrought and built.
If a man's mind hath evil thought,
pain comes on him as comes the wheel the ox behind.
If one endure in purity of thought,
Joy follows him as his own shadow - sure.

Man is a growth by law, and not a creation by artifice, and cause and effect are as absolute and undeviating in the hidden realm of thought as in the world of visible and material things. A noble and God-like character is not a thing of favor or chance, but is the natural result of continued effort in right thinking, the effect of long-cherished association with God-like thoughts. An ignoble and bestial character, by the same process, is the result of the continued harboring of groveling thoughts.

Man is made or unmade by himself. In the armory of thought he forges the weapons by which he destroys himself. He also fashions the tools with which he builds for himself heavenly mansions of joy and strength and peace. By the right choice and true application of thought, man ascends to the divine perfection. By the abuse and wrong application of thought he descends below the level of the beast.

Between these two extremes are all the grades of character, and man is their maker and master.

Of all the beautiful truths pertaining to the soul which have been restored and brought to light in this age, none is more gladdening or fruitful of divine promise and confidence than this--that man is the master of thought, the molder of character, and the maker and shaper of condition, environment, and destiny.

As a being of power, intelligence, and love, and the lord of his own thoughts, man holds the key to every situation, and contains within himself that transforming and regenerative agency by which he may make himself what he wills.

Man is always the master, even in his weakest and most abandoned state. But in his weakness and degradation he is foolish master who misgoverns his "household." When he begins to reflect upon his condition and search diligently for the law upon which his being is established, he then becomes the wise master, directing his energies with intelligence and fashioning his thoughts to fruitful issues. Such is the conscious master, and man can only thus become by discovering within himself the laws of thought. This discovery is totally a matter of application, self-analysis and experience.

Only by much searching and mining are gold and diamonds obtained, and man can find every truth connected with his being, if he will dig deep into the mine of his soul. That he is the maker of his character, the molder of his life, and the builder of his destiny, he may unerringly prove, if he will watch, control, and alter his thoughts, tracing their effects upon himself, upon others and upon his life and circumstances, linking cause and effect by patient practice and investigation. And utilizing his every experience, even the most trivial, everyday occurrence, as a means of obtaining that knowledge of himself which is understanding, wisdom, power. In this direction, as in no other, is the law absolute that "He that seeketh findeth; and to him that knocketh it shall be opened." For only by patience, practice, and ceaseless importunity can a man enter the door of the temple of knowledge.

Effect Of Thought On Circumstances

A man's mind may be likened to a garden, which may be intelligently cultivated or allowed to run wild; but whether cultivated or neglected, it must, and will bring forth. If no useful seeds are put into it, then an abundance of useless weed-seeds will fall therein, and will continue to produce their kind.

Just as a gardener cultivates his plot, keeping it free from weeds, and growing the flowers and fruits which he requires so may a man tend the garden of his mind, weeding out all the wrong, useless and impure thoughts, and cultivating toward perfection the flowers and fruits of right, useful and pure thoughts. By pursuing this process, a man sooner or later discovers that he is the master-gardener of his soul, the director of his life. He also reveals, within himself, the flaws of thought, and understands, with ever-increasing accuracy, how the thought-forces and mind elements operate in the shaping of character, circumstances, and destiny.

Thought and character are one, and as character can only manifest and discover itself through environment and circumstance, the outer conditions of a person's life will always be found to be harmoniously related to his inner state. This does not mean that a man's circumstances at any given time are an indication of his entire character, but that those circumstances are so intimately connected with some vital thought-element within himself that, for the time being, they are indispensable to his development.

Every man is where he is by the law of his being; the thoughts which he has built into his character have brought him there, and in the arrangement of his life there is no element of chance, but all is the result of a law which cannot err. This is just as true of those who feel "out of harmony" with their surroundings as of those who are contented with them.

As a progressive and evolving being, man is where he is that he may learn that he may grow; and as he learns the spiritual lesson which any circumstance contains for him, it passes away and gives place to other circumstances.

Man is buffeted by circumstances so long as he believes himself to be the creature of outside conditions, but when he realizes that he is a creative power, and that he may command the hidden soil and seeds of his being out of which circumstances grow; he then becomes the rightful master of himself.

That circumstances grow out of thought every man knows who has for any length of time practiced self-control and self-purification, for he will have noticed that the alteration in his circumstances has been in exact ratio with his altered mental condition. So true is this that when a man earnestly applies himself to remedy the defects in his character, and makes swift and marked progress, he passes rapidly through a succession of vicissitudes.

The soul attracts that which it secretly harbors, that which it loves, and also that which it fears. It reaches the height of its cherished aspirations; it falls to the level of its unchastened desires, and circumstances are the means by which the soul receives it own.

Every thought-seed sown or allowed to fall into the mind, and to take root there, produces its own, blossoming sooner or later into act, and bearing its own fruitage of opportunity and circumstance. Good thoughts bear good fruit, bad thoughts bad fruit.

The outer world of circumstances shapes itself to the inner world of thought, and both pleasant and unpleasant external conditions are factors which make for the ultimate good of the individual. As the reaper of his own harvest, man learns both of suffering and bliss.

Following the inmost desires, aspirations, thoughts, by which he allows himself to be dominated (pursuing the will-o'-the wisps of impure imaginings or steadfastly walking the highway of strong and high endeavor), a man at last arrives at their fruition and fulfillment in the outer conditions of his life. The laws of growth and adjustment everywhere obtain.

A man does not come to the alms-house or the jail by the tyranny of fate or circumstance, but by the pathway of groveling thoughts and base desires. Nor does a pure-minded man fall suddenly into crime by stress of any mere external force. The criminal thought had long been secretly fostered in the heart, and the hour of opportunity revealed its gathered power. Circumstance does not make the man; it reveals him to himself. No such conditions can exist as descending into vice and its attendant sufferings apart from vicious inclinations, or ascending into virtue and its pure happiness without the continued cultivation of virtuous aspirations; and man, therefore, as the lord and master of thought, is the maker of himself and the shaper of and author of environment. Even at birth the soul comes of its own and through every step of its earthly pilgrimage it attracts those combinations of conditions which reveal itself, which are the reflections of its own purity and impurity, its strength and weakness.

Men do not attract that which they want, but that which they are. Their whims, fancies, and ambitions are thwarted at every step, but their inmost thoughts and desires are fed with their own food, be it foul or clean. Man is manacled only by himself; thought and action are the jailors of Fate--they imprison, being base; they are also the angels of Freedom--they liberate, being noble. Not what he wished and prays for does a man get, but what he justly earns. His wishes and prayers are only gratified and answered when they harmonize with his thoughts and actions.

In the light of this truth what, then, is the meaning of "fighting against circumstances?" It means that a man is continually revolting against an effect without, while all the time he is nourishing and preserving its cause in his heart.

That cause may take the form of a conscious vice or an unconscious weakness; but whatever it is, it stubbornly retards the efforts of it possessor, and thus calls aloud for remedy.

Men are anxious to improve their circumstances, but are unwilling to improve themselves; they therefore remain bound. The man who does not shrink from self-crucifixion can never fail to accomplish the object upon which his heart is set. This is as true of earthly as of heavenly things. Even the man whose sole object is to acquire wealth must be prepared to make great personal sacrifices before he can accomplish his object; and how much more so he who would realize a strong and well-poised life?

Here is a man who is wretchedly poor. He is extremely anxious that his surroundings and home comforts should improve, yet all the time he shirks his work, and considers he is justified in trying to deceive his employer on the ground of the insufficiency of his wages. Such a man does not understand the simplest rudiments of those principles which are the basis of true prosperity, and is not only totally unfitted to rise out of his wretchedness, but is actually attracting to himself a still deeper wretchedness by dwelling in, and acting out, indolent, deceptive, and unmanly thoughts.

Here is a rich man who is the victim of a painful and persistent disease as the result of gluttony. He is willing to give large sums of money to get rid of it, but he will not sacrifice his gluttonous desires. He wants to gratify his taste for rich and unnatural foods and have his health as well. Such a man is totally unfit to have health, because he has not yet learned the first principles of a healthy life.

Here is an employer of labor who adopts crooked measures to avoid paying the regulation wage, and, in the hope of making larger profits, reduces the wages of his workpeople. Such a man is altogether unfitted for prosperity. And when he finds himself bankrupt, both as regards reputation and riches, he blames circumstances, not knowing that he is the sole author of his condition.

I have introduced these three cases merely as illustrative of the truth that man is the causer (though nearly always unconsciously) of his circumstances, and that, whilst aiming at the good end, he is continually frustrating its accomplishment by encouraging thoughts and desires which cannot possibly harmonize with that end. Such cases could be multiplied and varied almost indefinitely, but this is not necessary. The reader can, if he so resolves, trace the action of the laws of thought in his own mind and life, and until this is done, mere external facts cannot serve as a ground of reasoning.

Circumstances, however, are so complicated, thought is so deeply rooted, and the conditions of happiness vary so vastly with individuals, that a man's entire soul condition (although it may be known to himself) cannot be judged by another from the external aspect of his life alone.

A man may be honest in certain directions, yet suffer privations. A man may be dishonest in certain directions, yet acquire wealth. But the conclusion usually formed that the one man fails because of his particular honesty, and that the other prospers because of his particular dishonesty, is the result of a superficial judgment, which assumes that the dishonest man is almost totally corrupt, and honest man almost entirely virtuous. In the light of a deeper knowledge and wider experience, such judgment is found to be erroneous. The dishonest man may have some admirable virtues which the other does not possess; and the honest man obnoxious vices which are absent in the other. The honest man reaps the good results of his honest thoughts and acts; he also brings upon himself the sufferings which his vices produce. The dishonest man likewise garners his own suffering and happiness.

It is pleasing to human vanity to believe that one suffers because of one's virtue; but not until a man has extirpated every sickly, bitter, and impure thought from his soul, can he be in a position to know and declare that his sufferings are the result of his good, and not of his bad qualities; and on the way to, yet long before he has reached that supreme perfection , he will have found, working in his mind and life, the great law which is absolutely just, and which cannot, therefore, give good for evil, evil for good. Possessed of such knowledge, he will then know, looking back upon his past ignorance and blindness, that his life is, and always was, justly ordered, and that all his past experiences, good and bad, were the equitable outworking of his evolving, yet unevolved self.

Good thoughts and actions can never produce bad results; bad thoughts and actions can never produce good results. This is but saying that nothing can come from corn but corn, nothing from nettles but nettles. Men understand this law in the natural world, and work with it; but few understand it in the mental and moral world (though its operation there is just as simple and undeviating), and they, therefore, do not cooperate with it.

Suffering is always the effect of wrong thought in some direction. It is an indication that the individual is out of harmony with himself, with the law of his being. The sole and supreme use of suffering is to purify, to burn out all that is useless and impure. Suffering ceases for him who is pure. There could be no object in burning gold after the dross had been removed, and a perfectly pure and enlightened being could not suffer.

The circumstances which a man encounters with suffering are the result of his own mental inharmony. The circumstances which a man encounters with blessedness are the result of his own mental harmony. Blessedness, not material possessions, is the measure of right thought; wretchedness, not lack of material possessions, is the measure of wrong thought. A man may be cursed and rich; he may be blessed and poor. Blessedness and riches are only joined together when the riches are rightly and wisely used. And the poor man only descends into wretchedness when he regards his lot as a burden unjustly imposed.

Indigence and indulgence are the two extremes of wretchedness. They are both equally unnatural and the result of mental disorder. A man is not rightly conditioned until he is a happy, healthy, and prosperous being; and happiness, health, and prosperity are the result of a harmonious adjustment of the inner with the outer of the man with his surroundings.

A man only begins to be a man when he ceases to whine and revile, and commences to search for the hidden justice which regulates his life. And he adapts his mind to that regulating factor, he ceases to accuse others as the cause of his condition, and builds himself up in strong and noble thoughts; ceases to kick against circumstances, but begins to use them as aids to his more rapid progress, and as a means of discovering the hidden powers and possibilities within himself.

Law, not confusion, is the dominating principle in the universe; justice, not injustice, is the soul and substance of life. Righteousness, not corruption, is the molding and moving force in the spiritual government of the world. This being so, man has but to right himself to find that the universe is right. And during the process of putting himself right, he will find that as he alters his thoughts towards things and other people, things and other people will alter towards him.

The proof of this truth is in every person, and it therefore admits of easy investigation by systematic introspection and self-analysis. Let a man radically alter his thoughts, and he will be astonished at the rapid transformation it will effect in the material conditions of his life. Men imagine that thought can be kept secret, but it cannot. It rapidly crystallizes into habit, and habit solidifies into circumstance. Bestial thoughts crystallize into habits of drunkenness and sensuality, which solidify into circumstances of destitution and disease. Impure thoughts of every kind crystallize into enervating and confusing habits, which solidify into distracting and adverse circumstances. Thoughts of fear, doubt, and indecision crystallize into weak, unmanly, and irresolute habits, which solidify into circumstances of failure, indigence, and slavish dependence. Lazy thoughts crystallize into weak, habits of uncleanliness and dishonesty, which solidify into circumstances of foulness and beggary. Hateful and condemnatory thoughts crystallize into habits of accusation and violence, which solidify into circumstances of injury and persecution. Selfish thoughts of all kinds crystallize into habits of self-seeking, which solidify into distressful circumstances.

On the other hand, beautiful thoughts of all kinds crystallize into habits of grace and kindliness, which solidify into genial and sunny circumstances. Pure thoughts crystallize into habits of temperance and self-control, which solidify into circumstances of repose and peace. Thoughts of courage, self-reliance, and decision crystallize into manly habits, which solidify into circumstances of success, plenty, and freedom. Energetic thoughts crystallize into habits of cleanliness and industry, which solidify into circumstances of pleasantness. Gentle and forgiving thoughts crystallize into habits of gentleness, which solidify into protective and preservative circumstances. Loving and unselfish thoughts which solidify into circumstances of sure and abiding prosperity and true riches.

A particular train of thought persisted in, be it good or bad, cannot fail to produce its results on the character and circumstances. A man cannot directly choose his circumstances, but he can choose his thoughts, and so indirectly, yet surely, shape his circumstances.

Nature helps every man to gratification of the thoughts which he most encourages, and opportunities are presented which will most speedily bring to the surface both the good and the evil thoughts.

Let a man cease from his sinful thoughts, and all the world will soften towards him, and be ready to help him. Let him put away his weakly and sickly thoughts, and the opportunities will spring up on every hand to aid his strong resolves. Let him encourage good thoughts, and no hard fate shall bind him down to wretchedness and shame. The world is your kaleidoscope, and the varying combinations of colors which at every succeeding moment it presents to you are the exquisitely adjusted pictures of your ever-moving thoughts.

You will be what you will to be;
Let failure find its false content
In that poor word, "environment,"
But spirit scorns it, and is free.

It masters time, it conquers space;
It cows that boastful trickster, Chance,
And bids the tyrant Circumstance
Uncrown, and fill a servant's place.

The human Will, that force unseen,
The offspring of deathless Soul,
Can hew a way to any goal,
Though walls of granite intervene.

Be not impatient in delay,
But wait as one who understands;
When spirit rises and commands,
The gods are ready to obey.

Effects Of Thoughts
On Health And Body

The body is the servant of the mind. It obeys the operations of the mind, whether they be deliberately chosen or automatically expressed. At the bidding of unlawful thoughts the body sinks rapidly into disease and decay; at the command of glad and beautiful thoughts it becomes clothed with youthfulness and beauty.

Disease and health, like circumstances, are rooted in thought. Sickly thoughts will express themselves through a sickly body. Thoughts of fear have been known to kill a man as speedily as a bullet and they are continually killing thousands of people just as surely though less rapidly. The people who live in fear of disease are the people who get it. Anxiety quickly demoralizes the whole body, and lays it open to the entrance of disease; while impure thoughts, even if not physically indulged, will sooner shatter the nervous system.

Strong, pure, and happy thoughts build up the body in vigor and grace. The body is a delicate and plastic instrument, which responds readily to the thoughts by which it is impressed, and habits of thought will produce their own effects, good or bad, upon it.

Men will continue to have impure and poisoned blood, so long as they propagate unclean thoughts. Out of a clean heart comes a clean life and a clean body. Out of a defiled mind proceeds a defiled life and a corrupt body. Thought is the fount of action, life and manifestation; make the fountain pure, and all will be pure.

Change of diet will not help a man who will not change his thoughts. When a man makes his thoughts pure, he no longer desires impure food.

Clean thoughts make clean habits. The so-called saint who does not wash his body is not a saint. He who has strengthened and purified his thoughts does not need to consider the malevolent.

If you would perfect your body, guard your mind. If you would renew your body, beautify your mind. Thoughts of malice, envy, and disappointment, despondency, rob the body of its health and grace. A sour face does not come by chance; it is made by sour thoughts. Wrinkles that mar are drawn by folly, passion, pride.

I know a woman of ninety-six who has the bright, innocent face of a girl. I know a man well under middle age whose face is drawn into in harmonious contours. The one is the result of a sweet and sunny disposition; the other is the outcome of passion and discontent.

As you cannot have a sweet and wholesome abode unless you admit the air and sunshine freely into your rooms, so a strong body and a bright, happy, or serene countenance can only result from the free admittance into the mind of thoughts of joy and goodwill and serenity.

On the faces of the aged there are wrinkles made by sympathy others by strong and pure thought, and others are carved by passion; who cannot distinguish them? With those who have lived righteously, age is calm, peaceful, and softly mellowed, like the setting sun. I have recently seen a philosopher on his death-bed. He was not old except in years. He died as sweetly and peaccfully as he had lived.

There is no physician like cheerful thought for dissipating the ills of the body; there is no comforter to compare with goodwill for dispersing the shadows of grief and sorrow. To live continually in thoughts of ill-will, cynicism, suspicion, and envy, is to be confined in a self-made prison hole. But to think well of all, to be cheerful with all, to patiently learn to find the good in all--such unselfish thoughts are the very portals of heaven; and to dwell day by day in thoughts of peace toward every creature will bring abounding peace to their possessor.

Thought And Purpose

Until thought is linked with purpose there is no intelligent accomplishment. With the majority the bark of thought is allowed to "drift" upon the ocean of life. Aimlessness is a vice, and such drifting must not continue for him who would steer clear of catastrophe and destruction.

They who have no central purpose in their life fall an easy prey to petty worries, fears, troubles, and self-pityings, all of which are indications of weakness, which lead, just as surely as deliberately planned sins (though by a different route), to failure, unhappiness, and loss, for weakness cannot persist in a power-evolving universe.

A man should conceive of a legitimate purpose in his heart, and set out to accomplish it. He should make this purpose the centralizing point of his thoughts. It may take the form of a spiritual ideal, or it may be a worldly object, according to his nature at the time being. Whichever it is, he should steadily focus his thought-forces upon the object he had set before him. He should make this purpose his supreme duty and should devote himself to its attainment, not allowing his thoughts to wander away into ephemeral fancies, longings, and imaginings. This is the royal road to self-control and true concentration of thought. Even if he fails again and again to accomplish his purpose-- as he must until weakness is overcome--the strength of character gained will be the measure of his true success, and this will form a new starting point for future power and triumph.

Those who are not prepared for the apprehension of a great purpose, should fix the thoughts upon the faultless performance of their duty, no matter how insignificant their task may appear. Only in this way can the thoughts be gathered and focused, and resolution and energy be developed. Once this is done, there is nothing which may not be accomplished.

The weakest soul knowing its own weakness, and believing this truth--that strength can only be developed by effort and practice--will, thus believing, at once begin to exert itself. And, adding effort to effort, patience to patience, and strength to strength, will never cease to develop and will at last grow divinely strong.

As the physically weak man can make himself strong by careful and patient training, so the man of weak thoughts can make them strong by exercising himself in right thinking.

To put away aimlessness and weakness and to begin to think with purpose is to enter the ranks of those strong ones who only recognize failure as one of the pathways to attainment. Who make all conditions serve them, and who think strongly, attempt fearlessly, and accomplish masterfully.

Having conceived of his purpose, a man should mentally mark out a straight pathway to its achievement, looking neither to the right nor left. Doubts and fears should be rigorously excluded. They are disintegrating elements which break up the straight line of effort, rendering it crooked, ineffectual, useless. Thoughts of doubt and fear can never accomplish anything. They always lead to failure. Purpose, energy, power to do, and all strong thoughts cease when doubt and fear creep in.

The will to do springs from the knowledge that we can do. Doubt and fear are the great enemies of knowledge, and he who encourages them, who does not slay them, thwarts himself at every step.

He who has conquered doubt and fear has conquered failure. His every thought is allied with power, and all difficulties are bravely met and overcome. His purposes are seasonably planted, and they bloom and bring forth fruit that does not fall prematurely to the ground.

Thought allied fearlessly to purpose becomes creative force. He who knows this is ready to become something higher and stronger than a bundle of wavering thoughts and fluctuating sensations. He who does this has become the conscious and intelligent wielder of his mental powers.

The Thought-Factor In Achievement

All that a man achieves and all that he fails to achieve is the direct result of his own thoughts. In a justly ordered universe, where loss of equipoise would mean total destruction, individual responsibility must be absolute. A man's weakness and strength, purity and impurity, are his own and not another man's. They are brought about by himself and not by another; and they can only be altered by himself, never by another. His condition is also his own, and not another man's. His sufferings and his happiness are evolved from within. As he thinks, so is he; as he continues to think, so he remains.

A strong man cannot help a weaker unless that weaker is willing to be helped. And even then the weak man must become strong of himself. He must, by his own efforts, develop the strength which he admires in another. None but himself can alter his condition.

It has been usual for men to think and to say, "Many men are slaves because one is an oppressor; let us hate the oppressor!" But there is amongst an increasing few a tendency to reverse this judgment and to say, "One man is an oppressor because many are slaves; let us despise the slaves."

The truth is that oppressor and slaves are cooperators in ignorance, and, while seeming to afflict each other, are in reality, afflicting themselves. A perfect knowledge perceives the action of law in the weakness of the oppressed and the misapplied power of the oppressor. A perfect love, seeing the suffering which both states entail, condemns neither; a perfect compassion embraces both oppressor and oppressed. He who has conquered weakness and has pushed away all selfish thoughts belongs neither to oppressor nor oppressed. He is free.

A man can only rise, conquer, and achieve by lifting up his thoughts. He can only remain weak, abject, and miserably by refusing to lift up his thoughts.

Before a man can achieve anything, even in worldly things, he must lift his thoughts above slavish animal indulgence. He may not, in order to succeed, give up all animality and selfishness, necessarily, but a portion of it must, at least, be sacrificed. A man whose first thought is bestial indulgence could neither think clearly nor plan methodically. He could not find and develop his latent resources and would fail in any undertaking. Not having begun to manfully control his thoughts, he is not in a position to control affairs and to adopt serious responsibilities.

He is not fit to act independently and stand alone. But he is limited only by the thoughts that he chooses.

There can be no progress nor achievement without sacrifice, and a man's worldly success will be by the measure that he sacrifices his confused animal thoughts, and fixes his mind on the development of his plans, and the strengthening of his resolution and self-reliance. The higher he lifts his thoughts, the greater will be his success, the more blessed and enduring will be his achievements.

The universe does not favor the greedy, the dishonest, the vicious, although on the mere surface it sometimes may appear to do so. It helps the honest, the magnanimous, the virtuous. All the great teachers of the ages have declared this in varying ways, and to prove it and to know it a man has but to persist in making himself increasingly virtuous by lifting his thoughts.

Intellectual achievements are the result of thought consecrated to the search for knowledge or for the beautiful and true in nature. Such achievements may sometimes be connected with vanity and ambition, but they are not the outcome of those characteristics. They are the natural outgrowth of long and arduous effort, and of pure and unselfish thoughts.

Spiritual achievements are the consummation of holy aspirations. He who lives constantly in the conception of noble and lofty thoughts, who dwells upon all that is pure and selfless, will, as surely as the sun reaches its zenith and the moon its full, become wise and noble in character and rise into a position of influence and blessedness. Achievement of any kind is the crown of effort, the diadem of thought. By the aid of self-control, resolution, purity, righteousness, and well-directed thought a man ascends. By the aid of animality, indolence, impurity, corruption, and confusion of thought a man descends.

A man may rise to high success in the world, even to lofty attitudes in the spiritual realm, and again descend into weakness and wretchedness by allowing arrogant, selfish, and corrupt thoughts to take possession of him.

Victories attained by right thought can be maintained only by watchfulness. Many give way when success is assured, and rapidly fall back into failure.

All achievements, whether in the business, intellectual, or spiritual world, are the result of definitely directed thought. They are governed by the same law, and are of the same method. The only difference lies in the object of attainment.

He who would accomplish little need sacrifice little; he who would achieve much must sacrifice much. He who would attain highly must sacrifice greatly.

Visions And Ideals

The dreamers are the saviors of the world. As the visible world is sustained by the invisible, so men, through all their trials and sins and sordid vocations, are nourished by the beautiful visions of their solitary dreamers. Humanity cannot forget its dreamers; it cannot let their ideals fade and die; it lives in them; it knows them as the realities which it shall one day see and know.

Composer, sculptor, painter, poet, prophet, sage--these are the makers of the after-world, the architects of heaven. The world is beautiful because they have lived. Without them, laboring humanity would perish.

He who cherishes a beautiful vision, a lofty ideal in his heart, will one day realize it. Columbus cherished a vision of another world and he discovered it. Copernicus fostered the vision of a multiplicity of worlds and a wider universe, and he revealed it. Buddha beheld the vision of a spiritual world of stainless beauty and perfect peace, and he entered into it.

Cherish your visions; cherish your ideals. Cherish the music that stirs in your heart, the beauty that forms in your mind, the loveliness that drapes your purest thoughts. For out of them will grow all delightful conditions, all heavenly environment; of these, if you but remain true to them, your world will at last be built.

To desire is to obtain; to aspire is to achieve. Shall man's basest desires receive the fullest measure of gratification, and his purest aspirations starve for lack of sustenance? Such is not the Law. Such a condition can never obtain, "Ask and receive."

Dream lofty dreams, and as you dream, so shall you become. Your vision is the promise of what you shall one day be; your ideal is the prophecy of what you shall at last unveil.

The greatest achievement was at first and for a time a dream. The oak sleeps in the acorn; the bird waits in the egg. And in the highest vision of a soul a waking angel stirs. Dreams are the seedlings of realities.

Your circumstances may be uncongenial, but they shall not remain so if you only perceive an ideal and strive to reach it. You cannot travel within and stand still without. Here is a youth hard pressed by poverty and labor. Confined long hours in an unhealthy workshop; unschooled and lacking all the arts of refinement. But he dreams of better things.

He thinks of intelligence, or refinement, of grace and beauty. He conceives of, mentally builds up, an ideal condition of life. The wider liberty and a larger scope takes possession of him; unrest urges him to action, and he uses all his spare times and means to the development of his latent powers and resources. Very soon so altered has his mind become that the workshop can no longer hold him. It has become so out of harmony with his mind-set that it falls out of his life as a garment is cast aside. And with the growth of opportunities that fit the scope of his expanding powers, he passes out of it altogether. Years later we see this youth as a grown man. We find him a master of certain forces of the mind that he wields with worldwide influence and almost unequaled power. In his hands he holds the cords of gigantic responsibilities; he speaks and lives are changed; men and women hang upon his words and remold their characters. Sun-like, he becomes the fixed and luminous center around which innumerable destinies revolve. He has realized the vision of his youth. He has become one with his ideal.

And you, too, will realize the vision (not just the idle wish) of your heart, be it base or beautiful, or a mixture of both; for you will always gravitate toward that which you secretly love most. Into your hands will be placed the exact results of your own thoughts. You will receive that which you earn; no more, no less. Whatever your present environment may be, you will fall, remain, or rise with your thoughts-- your vision, your ideal. You will become as small as your controlling desire, as great as your dominant aspiration.

The thoughtless, the ignorant, and the indolent, seeing only the apparent effects of things and not the things themselves, talk of luck, of fortune, and chance. Seeing a man grow rich, they say, "How lucky he is!" Observing another become skilled intellectually, they exclaim, "How highly favored he is!" And noting the saintly character and wide influence of another, they remark, "How chance helps him at every turn!" They do not see the trials and failures and struggles which these men have encountered in order to gain their experience. They have no knowledge of the sacrifices they have made, of the undaunted efforts they have put forth, of the faith they have exercised so that they might overcome the apparently insurmountable and realize the vision of their heart. They do not know the darkness and the heartaches; they only see the light and joy, and call it "luck." Do not see the long, arduous journey, but only behold the pleasant goal and call it "good fortune." Do not understand the process, but only perceive the result, and call it "chance."

In all human affairs there are efforts, and there are results. The strength of the effort is the measure of the result. Chance is not. Gifts, powers, material, intellectual, and spiritual possessions are the fruits of effort. They are thoughts completed, objectives accomplished, visions realized.

The vision that you glorify in your mind, the ideal that you enthrone in your heart -- this you will build your life by; this you will become.

Serenity

Calmness of mind is one of the beautiful jewels of wisdom. It is the result of long and patient effort in self-control. Its presence is an indication of ripened experience, and of a more than ordinary knowledge of the laws and operations of thought.

A man becomes calm in the measure that he understands himself as a thought-evolved being. For such knowledge necessitates the understanding of others as the result of thought, and as he develops a right understanding, and sees ever more clearly the internal relations of things by the action of cause and effect, he ceases to fuss, fume, worry, and grieve. He remains poised, steadfast, serene.

The calm man, having learned how to govern himself, knows how to adapt himself to others. And they, in turn reverence his spiritual strength. They feel that they can learn from him and rely upon him. The more tranquil a man becomes, the greater is his success, his influence, his power for good. Even the ordinary trader will find his business prosperity increase as he develops a greater self-control and equanimity, for people will always prefer to deal with a man whose demeanor is equitable.

The strong, calm man is always loved and revered. He is like a shade-giving tree in a thirsty land, or a sheltering rock in a storm. Who does not love a tranquil heart, a sweet-tempered, balanced life? It does not matter whether it rains or shines, or what changes come to those who possess these blessings, for they are always serene and calm. That exquisite poise of character that we call serenity is the last lesson of culture. It is the flowering of life, the fruitage of the soul. It is precious as wisdom--more desirable than fine gold. How insignificant mere money-seeking looks in comparison with a serene life. A life that dwells in the ocean of truth, beneath the waves, beyond the reach of the tempests, in the Eternal Calm!

How many people we know who sour their lives, who ruin all that is sweet and beautiful by explosive tempers, who destroy their poise of character and make bad blood! It is a question whether the great majority of people do not ruin their lives and mar their happiness by lack of self-control. How few people we meet in life who are well balanced, who have that exquisite poise which is characteristic of the finished character!

Yes, humanity surges with uncontrolled passion, is tumultuous with ungoverned grief, is blown about by anxiety and doubt. Only the wise man, only he whose thoughts are controlled and purified, makes the winds and the storms of the soul obey him.

Tempest-tossed souls, wherever you may be, under whatever conditions you may live, know this: In the ocean of life the isles of blessedness are smiling and the sunny shore of your ideal awaits your coming. Keep your hands firmly upon the helm of thought. In the core of your soul reclines the commanding Master; He does but sleep; wake Him. Self-control is strength. Right thought is mastery. Calmness is power. Say unto your heart, "Peace. Be still!"

SYLVIA'S
FOUNDATION INC.

Sylvia Murphy Fanelli was born in the hills of Kentucky in 1906. At age 26 she married Victor Fanelli, the son of recent Italian immigrants. Several years later they moved to rural North Central Florida which was to be her home until she passed away in 1976. Ten years after their marriage Victor suffered an appendicitis attack and soon died of complications.

The 36-year-old Sylvia suddenly found herself a young widow with five children under the age of ten. Living in her adopted state of Florida, she faced her challenge without the aid of a nearby family and without significant governmental assistance. She had an eighth-grade education, no skills, she never owned an automobile (and never had a driver's license). Despite her obstacles, she managed to raise five children into responsible and productive citizens while modeling an incredibly positive attitude --- it is an attitude that still lingers today among those who were touched by her.

Sylvia's Foundation, Inc. is a non-denominational, not-for-profit organization that was chartered in Florida in September 2002 and has been recognized by the IRS as a tax-exempt organization that meets 501 (c)(3) requirements (this means your contributions are fully tax-deductible as allowed by law). It is named in honor of Sylvia Murphy Fanelli and is dedicated to serving today's "Sylvias" and their families.

Our mission is to develop programs that will improve the quality of life and make a difference for young, widowed moms and their children. These programs include educational aid and stipends and automobile and home ownership assistance grants.

Please see our website at **www.Sylvias-Love.org** or write us at:

Sylvia's Foundation Inc.
PO Box 2087
St Augustine FL 32085 USA